WHOSE NOSE IS THIS?

¿DE QUIÉN ES ESTA NARIZ?

JOANNE RANDOLPH

TRADUCCIÓN AL ESPAÑOL:
MA. PILAR OBREGÓN

PowerKiDS & Editorial Buenas Letras™
press

Published in 2009 by The Rosen Publishing Group, Inc.
29 East 21st Street, New York, NY 10010

First Edition

Book Design: Julio Gil
Photo Researcher: Jessica Gerweck

Photo Credits: All images from Shutterstock.com.

Library of Congress Cataloging-in-Publication Data

Randolph, Joanne.
  [Whose nose is this? Spanish & English]
  Whose nose is this? = ¿De quién es esta nariz? / Joanne Randolph ; traducción al español,
  Ma. Pilar Obregón. – 1st ed.
      p. cm. – (Animal clues = ¿Adivina de quién es?)
  Includes index.
  ISBN 978-1-4358-2528-4 (library binding)
  1. Nose–Juvenile literature. I. Title. II. Title: ¿De quién es esta nariz?
  QL947.R3518 2009
  590–dc22
                                                        2007052077

Manufactured in the United States of America

Web Sites: Due to the changing nature of Internet links, PowerKids Press and Editorial Buenas Letras have developed an online list of Web sites related to the subject of this book. This site is updated regularly. Please use this link to access the list: www.powerkidslinks.com/acl/nose/

CONTENTS

CONTENIDO

Whose nose is long and gray?

¿Quién tiene una trompa larga de color gris?

An elephant's nose is long and gray.

La trompa del elefante es larga y de color gris.

Whose nose is black and **round**?

¿Quién tiene una nariz negra y **redonda**?

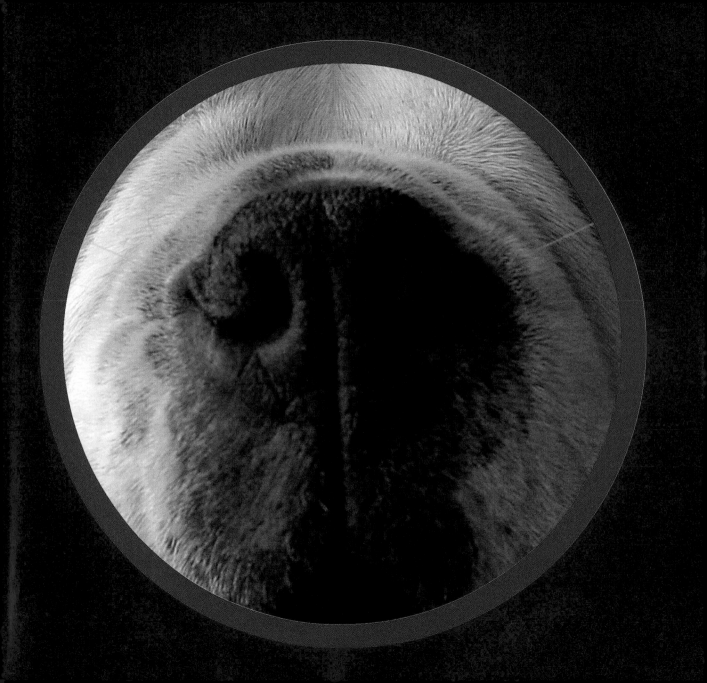

This bulldog's nose is black and round.

La nariz del bulldog es negra y redonda.

Which animal has a nose with two **pointy horns**?

¿Qué animal tiene dos **cuernos puntiagudos** en la nariz?

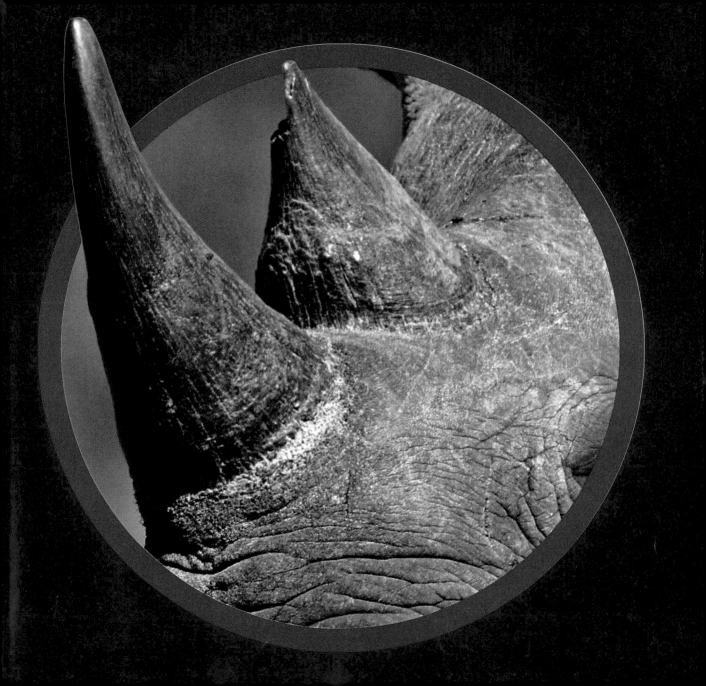

A rhino has a nose with two pointy horns.

El rinoceronte tiene dos cuernos puntiagudos en la nariz.

Whose nose is this, with its funny **folds**?

¿De quién es esta nariz con estos **pliegues** tan graciosos?

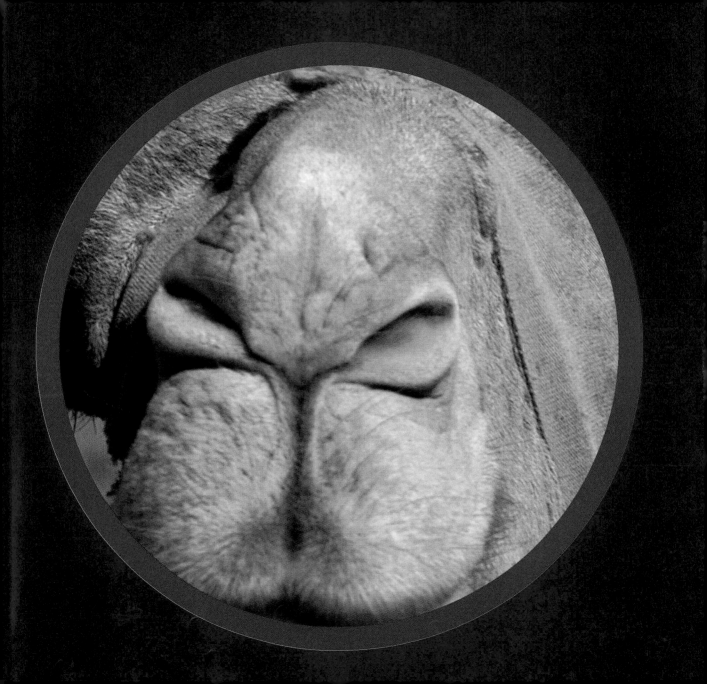

A camel belongs to this nose with the funny folds.

El camello tiene una nariz con pliegues graciosos.

Whose nose has holes that sit on top?

¿Qué animal tiene agujeros en la parte de arriba de la nariz?

A hippo's nose has holes that sit on top.

El hipopótamo tiene agujeros en la parte de arriba de la nariz.

WORDS TO KNOW · PALABRAS QUE DEBES SABER

folds / (los) pliegues

horns / (los) cuernos

pointy / puntiagudo

round / redondo

INDEX

A
animal, 12

C
camel, 18

F
folds, 16, 18

H
horns, 12, 14

ÍNDICE

A
animal, 12

C
camello, 18
cuernos, 12, 14

P
pliegues, 16, 18